Knitting with Gigi

By Karen Thalacker

Illustrated by Mindy Dwyer

Includes step-by-step instructions and 8 patterns

acknowledgments

Knitting with Gigi has taken me on an unexpected and wonderful journey. My heartfelt thanks go to: Mary Green and the entire Martingale family for bringing Gigi to life. Mindy Dwyer for her fabulous artwork, and Ellen Wheat for her skillful editing. Plymouth Yarn Company for their generous donation of yarn. My parents, family, and friends for their love and encouragement. Julie who taught me to knit and Greg who inspired me. Everyone at St. Paul's Lutheran School. And most of all, to Pete, Ella, Robby, Andy, and Malcolm. You mean everything to me.

Knitting with Gigi
© 2007 by Karen Thalacker
Illustrations © 2007 by Mindy Dwyer

Martingale®
& COMPANY

Martingale & Company
20205 144th Avenue NE
Woodinville, WA 98072-8478 USA
www.martingale-pub.com

Printed in China
12 11 10 09 08 07   8 7 6 5 4 3 2 1

Library of Congress Cataloging-In-Publication Data
Library of Congress Control Number: 2006035736
ISBN-13: 978-1-56477-758-4

Mission Statement
Dedicated to providing quality products and service to inspire creativity.

President: Nancy J. Martin
CEO: Daniel J. Martin
COO: Tom Wierzbicki
Publisher: Jane Hamada
Editorial Director: Mary V. Green
Managing Editor: Tina Cook
Design Director: Stan Green
Project Manager: Ellen Wheat
Cover and Text Designer: Elizabeth Watson
Copy Editor: Sheila Chapman Ryan

3 1907 00204 1647

Visit www.gigiknits.com for more!

Contents

gigi's gift   4

learning to knit   6

Let's get started   7

What you'll need   8

How to make a yarn ball   9

How to make a slipknot and cast on   10

How to do the knit stitch   12

How to decrease   14

How to start a new yarn ball or color   15

How to bind off   16

How to sew a seam   17

How to weave in ends   18

How to fix mistakes   19

patterns   20

Pot holder   21

Belt   22

Baby blanket   23

Scarves   24

Wrist warmers   26

Bag   28

Hat   30

knitting to help others   32

gigi's gift

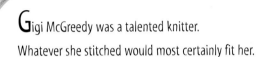

Gigi McGreedy was a talented knitter.
Whatever she stitched would most certainly fit her.

Gigi knit colorful mittens and muffs,
And soft cozy slippers and sweaters with cuffs.

Pants for her dog and a coat for her cat,
A gown for her guppy—well, how about that?

Her closet was cluttered, her room was crammed full
With special creations of cotton and wool.

A mountain of yarn was approaching the ceiling
When Mom had to tell her just how she was feeling.

"Enough is enough," her mom gently said.
"Have you thought of knitting for others instead?"

Gigi replied, "That sure would be new,
But would it be something a child could do?"

"Your gift," her mom said, "was meant to be shared.
Sad folks might be glad if they knew someone cared."

Deep down inside, Gigi knew that was right.
So she got out her needles and yarn that was bright.

She knit for her cousin whose tonsils were red.
And then for a teacher at home sick in bed.

She knit for her coach who was feeling real blue.
And then for a pal who was down with the flu.

Each stitch was a prayer that the sick would feel better.
That their chill would be gone when they put on her sweater.

4

But she also knew there was much more to do,
If one person could help, then how about two?

If two people could help, then possibly four
Could assemble more friends and knit even more.

She gathered them all so that work could be done,
And showed them that crafting for others was fun.

She taught them to cast on, to knit, and sew seams.
They learned to serve others and work as a team.

They knit for the nursery with needles a-flying,
Creating soft hats to keep babies from crying.

They knit little sweaters for kids in far lands,
And hats for the homeless who needed a hand.

They knit scarves for sailors, who tour far and wide,
And socks for our soldiers who serve us with pride.

Their stitching continued for weeks and for years.
For the spirited knitters, the message was clear:

Open your hearts to the troubles of neighbors,
And lighten their load with the fruits of your labors.

True acts of kindness are pleasing to do.
Gigi McGreedy helps others—how about you?

5

learning to knit

Gigi McGreedy will teach you to knit.
She'll patiently help you to learn bit by bit.

Up through the stitch, put the yarn through the middle,
Down through the same stitch, and little by little

You'll get less clumsy as you try but still fumble,
Working with needles and yarn in a jumble.

In no time at all, you'll be stitching in bliss.
But when projects get tough, just remember this:

"Practice makes perfect" will never apply.
We all make mistakes, no matter how hard we try.

So be of good cheer and do not despair.
With time and some care, you'll have something to wear.

Gigi has faith in what you can do.
Your knitting is special—just like you.

6

Let's get started

I'm so glad you want to learn to knit!

I remember when I learned how to knit. It felt kind of awkward at first. My Grandma said that, with a little practice, my hands would learn to work together. She was right! I was knitting in no time! Now I knit almost everywhere—in the car, on the bus, and even at the beach. The yarn feels so good against my fingers as my needles click away.

My friends and I have tons of fun together when we knit, and I can't wait for you to join us.

You'll love all the neat things you can make!

All you need for knitting fits in a bag.

One of the reasons knitting is such a cool hobby is that you don't need much equipment to get started. Besides a bag to put it all in, you just need knitting needles, yarn, scissors, a yarn needle, a crochet hook, and this book. To get your materials, go to a craft store or your local yarn store. They will be happy to help you. Just tell them you need size 8 needles and some worsted-weight yarn. You'll want a small, sharp pair of scissors, and the crochet hook should be about size 5. For the practice project in this book, I used worsted-weight yarn in a light color. For most of the patterns in the book, any worsted-weight yarn will do.

To do all of the projects in this book, you only need to learn a few basic knitting skills. I'm going to explain each of them to you, one by one. We'll take it a step at a time. If there is any part you can't figure out, go online and check out my Web site at www.gigiknits.com. There you will find all sorts of helpful information. You could also take a trip to your local yarn store. There, other knitters will be glad to help you.

If you don't have a yarn store nearby, ask people at your church, school, library, or craft store.

There are knitters everywhere!

Why size 8 needles and worsted-weight yarn?

Why size 8 knitting needles? Knitting needles come in all materials, sizes, and colors. They can be thin or thick, short or long. They can be made of metal, plastic, or wood. The needle size is usually printed on the bottom or side of the needle. Size 8 needles are perfect for beginners because they aren't too thin or too thick. You can use them to do all of the projects in this book.

Why worsted-weight yarn in a light color for a practice project? Yarn comes in all weights, sizes, and colors. Yarn that is very thin is called "fingering" or "sport-weight" yarn. Yarn that is a little thicker than worsted weight is called "chunky." Worsted-weight yarn is thicker than sport weight but thinner than chunky weight. It's perfect for learning to knit. Try to get a light color when you're just getting started, because it's easier to see your stitches with light-colored yarn. Be sure to read the paper label wrapped around your yarn. It will tell you whether it's sport, bulky, or worsted-weight yarn. And it will also give you other information, like how to wash it.

How to make a yarn ball

Are you ready to begin?

We'll begin by winding your yarn into a ball. Most yarn comes in a skein. "Skein" rhymes with "plane." The first thing you need to do is find the beginning of the yarn, which is hidden deep in the center of the skein. A skein will sometimes have knots in it that you should undo before you start knitting. To get to the beginning "end" of the yarn, reach your fingers deep into the hole in the middle of the skein and pull it out. Can you see the beginning of the skein? Sometimes the yarn in the middle of the skein comes out in a tangled blob. Patiently sort through to find the beginning of the yarn.

Some yarn comes in a hank. A hank is wound looser than a skein and it is twisted to hold it in place. You can find the beginning of a hank by untying the loose knots that are holding it together. Have someone hold the hank in their hands while you wind your yarn ball, or do like I do and put it over the top of a chair.

Now you're ready to make a yarn ball:

1. Take the end of the yarn, and wrap it around your three fingers several times.

2. Take the wrapped yarn off your fingers, bunch it up, and continue to wrap the yarn, criss-crossing it around, again and again, making a ball shape. Wind the yarn loosely, so you don't stretch it.

3. Continue wrapping, making a yarn ball, until you reach the end of the skein.

Now we're ready to cast on!

After you wind the yarn into a ball, put the ball in a small plastic bag. It's easier to work with that way, and won't fall on the floor and roll all over.

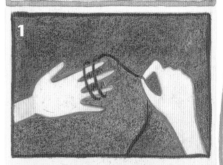

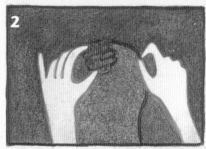

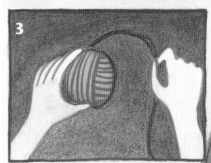

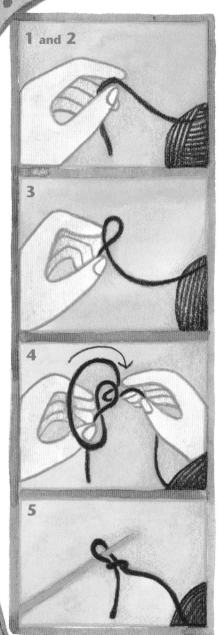

1 and 2

3

4

5

The first thing we need to do is make a slipknot.

Here's how to make a slipknot:

1. Grab the yarn about 8 inches from the end.

2. Pinch it between your thumb and index finger on your left hand.

3. Wrap the yarn loosely around your left index finger until it crosses.

4. With your right hand, grab the yarn about 4 inches from the short end, pull it around the back of the yarn, and slip the yarn into the hole created by your index finger, gently pulling it up. Don't pull the short end all of the way through. Instead make a little loop and gently tighten the yarn around it. You've just made a slipknot!

5. Now, place the slipknot onto a knitting needle: this is your first stitch. Make sure the stitch is snug on the needle but also loose enough to poke the other needle up through it. The slipknot is your first stitch on the needle.

If you've tried my instructions but can't make a slipknot, don't get discouraged. Just tie the yarn in any old loose knot and slip it on the needle. You can figure out how to make a slipknot later.

Visit www.gigiknits.com for helpful hints.

"Casting on" is how you get your stitches on the needle.

Now it's time to put more stitches on the needle. There are many different ways to cast on. I'll teach you one way, and after you've finished your practice project, you can go online and visit my Web site at www.gigiknits.com, to learn how to cast on a different way.

Here's how to cast on:

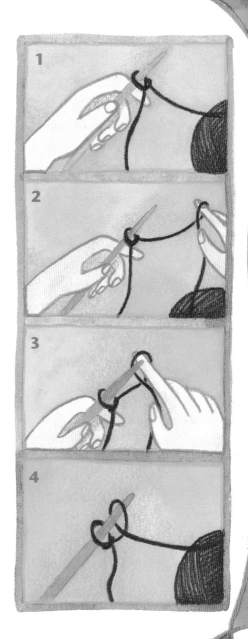

1. Hold the needle in your left hand. Leave the short end of the yarn hanging down— it's called the "tail," and you will weave it in at the end of the project.

2. With your right hand, take the yarn that's attached to the ball, and wrap it around your right index finger until it crosses.

3. Take your left needle and insert the tip up into the hole that's been created by your right index finger.

4. With the left needle, pull the stitch off your finger and onto the needle. Give the yarn a little tug to gently snug up the stitch on your left needle so that it's next to the first stitch, and not too loose and not too tight.

5. Repeat steps 1 through 4 until you have 15 stitches on your needle, including the slipknot.

It's time to start knitting!

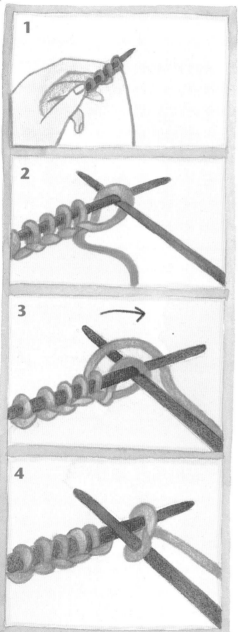

Our first project is just for practice.

Don't worry if you make mistakes in this practice project. We'll start a real project when you feel comfortable. When you're done with your practice project, you might want to keep it. Then, when you're knitting scarves and hats and other fun things, it will be a reminder that you worked hard to learn something new.

Here's how to do the knit stitch:

1. Hold the needle with the cast-on stitches in your left hand. The stitches should be toward the top of the left needle, right before the needle starts to get skinny. Place your left index finger gently on the left side of the top stitch on the left needle, to hold it in place.

2. Take the empty needle in your right hand and insert the tip through the top stitch and under the left needle.

3. With your right hand, take your yarn and bring it from the back to the front between the needles, and wrap it up around the point of your right needle.

4. With your index finger on your right hand, hold down the stitch on your right needle. Move the tip of the right needle down through the stitch on the left needle, bringing the right needle from the back to the front of the left needle. The two needles should look like an X, with your yarn still wrapped around your right needle.

That's all it takes—you're a knitter!

"Up, around, down, and off."

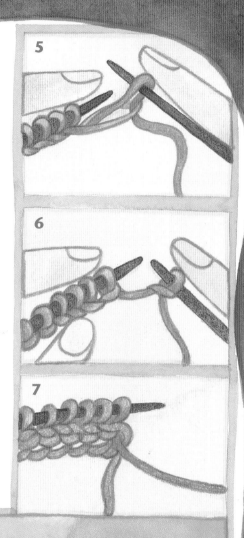

5. Gently scoot the stitch on the left needle up and off the needle.

6. Now you have 1 stitch on the right needle and 14 stitches on the left needle. Keeping your left index finger on the top stitch of the left needle, repeat steps 2 through 5 with the next stitch on the left needle. And then repeat steps 2 through 5 again with the rest of the stitches until you have just 1 stitch on the left needle. Knit that last stitch just like you knitted the rest. The left needle will be empty and all 15 stitches will be on your right needle.

7. Put the needle with all the stitches in your left hand. Smooth out the stitches on the needle so they are not twisted. Make sure the tail and the yarn you are knitting with are both below the left needle.

8. Start with step 2 and repeat, knitting rows until you feel comfortable. It may take 10 rows or 20 rows or 30 or even 40.

Don't worry—you will get it!

Up, around, down, and off.

Here's a helpful hint. I remember how to do the knit stitch by saying, "Up, around, down, and off." "**Up**" is for step 2, when you insert the tip of the right needle into the stitch on the left needle. "**Around**" is for when you bring the yarn from the back through the middle in step 3. "**Down**" is for step 4, when you move the tip of the right needle down through the stitch on the left needle and you make an X with the right needle and left needle. "**Off**" is for when you scoot the stitch off the left needle. "Up, around, down, and off."

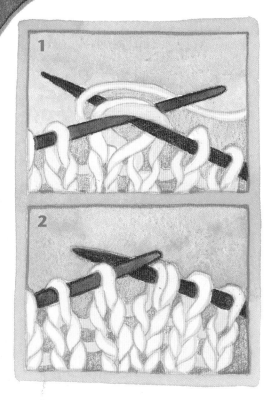

Learning to decrease can be fun!

Sometimes you need to get rid of some of the stitches on your needle to make something smaller or give it a special shape. The easiest way to get rid of stitches, or decrease, is called "knit 2 together," or "k2tog" for short.

Here's how to decrease:

1. Put your right needle into the top 2 stitches on your left needle. Knit them just like when you're knitting 1 stitch.

2. When you knit 2 stitches together instead of separately, you've decreased or gotten rid of 1 stitch.

Easy huh?!

What is the garter stitch?

The "garter stitch" is the knitting pattern that is made by knitting every stitch of every row. Every 2 rows you knit will form 1 ridge. This makes it easy to keep track of how many rows you've done. If you count 10 ridges, you've knit 20 rows. If you want to knit a square using the garter stitch, the number of ridges should equal the number of stitches you cast on. For example, if you cast on 25 stitches, you will knit 25 ridges (or 50 rows) to make a square.

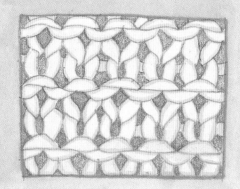

Want to change colors or start a new ball of yarn?

When you're working on a project, you may want to change colors or start a new ball of yarn. Start a new yarn ball or color at the beginning of a row, so that the new row looks even when your project is finished. If you're getting close to the end of a ball of yarn, make sure you've got enough to finish the row.

Here's how you start a new yarn ball:

1. Insert the tip of the right needle into the first stitch on the left needle.

2. Hold the yarn from the new ball about 8 inches from the beginning, and bring it from back to front between the needles.

3. Knit the first stitch on your left needle with the new yarn.

4. You will have 2 tails at the top of your left needle—one of the old yarn and one of the new yarn. Gently tug on the 2 tails to tighten them so they don't come undone. If you're worried about them unraveling, tie the tails together in a loose knot. When your project is finished, you can untie them and weave in the ends.

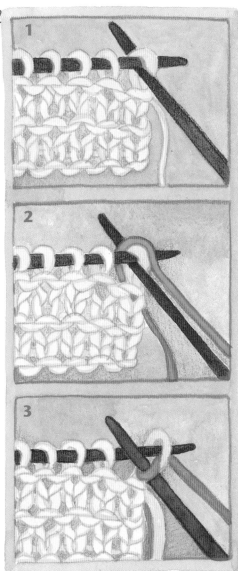

That's all there is to it!

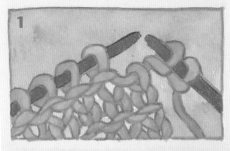

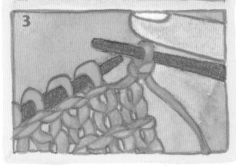

Finishing a project is so exciting!

When you're done knitting, it's time to bind off. "Binding off" or "casting off" is what you do to make sure that your final stitches are woven into the knitted edge so your project won't unravel.

Here's how to bind off:

1. Knit each of the two top stitches from the left needle onto the right needle.

2. With your left knitting needle, gently pull the lower stitch on your right needle, or the first stitch you knitted, up and over the second stitch you knitted.

3. Then scoot the first stitch off the left needle, so that you have 1 stitch remaining on the right needle. It may help to keep your right index finger on the top stitch to keep it from accidentally falling off when you're pulling the first stitch over it.

4. Knit 1 stitch onto your right needle. Repeat steps 2 through 4 until you have only 1 stitch remaining on your right needle.

5. Cut your yarn, leaving an 8- to 12-inch tail. Carefully pull the tail through the last stitch, and pull it gently to secure it.

Good job! Your final stitches are safe, and even the most playful cat won't be able to unravel them.

How to sew a seam

After binding off, it's time to use your yarn needle!

If you're making a project like a hat or purse, you will need to sew up the side seams at the end. To sew up a knitted seam, you'll use your yarn needle.

Here's how I sew up a seam:

1. Put the seams you want to sew side by side, with the right sides out, or facing you. Line up the garter-stitch ridges on each side of the seam.

2. Thread your yarn needle with a leftover piece of yarn from your project. (See page 18 for a trick for threading your needle.)

3. Coming from the inside of your project, bring the needle up through the bottom loop on both sides. Pull the needle gently to tighten.

4. On the next ridge up, bring the needle through the loop on one side.

5. Still working on the front, find the matching ridge on the other side of the seam and bring the yarn through the loop. Gently tighten the yarn.

6. Sew the yarn back and forth like this through each garter-stitch ridge. Be sure to check the seam often to make sure your sewing isn't too tight or too loose.

7. When you get to the end of the seam, check to make sure there are no holes in your seam. If you find one, turn your project inside out and mend the hole with the yarn on your yarn needle.

Just take your time, and your project will look great!

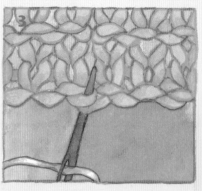

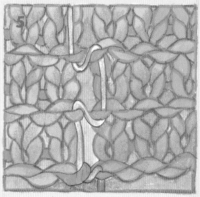

Look on my Web site for a short video on how to sew a seam.

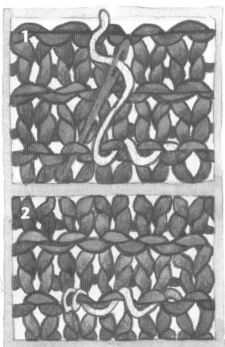

This is fun!

Weaving in the ends is the last thing you do to finish a knitting project. We weave in the ends so they won't unravel when you're wearing the item or washing it. To weave in the ends, turn the object inside out, and work on the back side.

Here's how to weave in ends:

1. Put the tail end of your yarn through the eye of the needle.

2. On the back side of the project, carefully sew the yarn through several stitches.

3. When you have done that on several stitches, secure the yarn end by weaving it around the final stitch a few times, creating a sort of a knot. Cut the remaining tail.

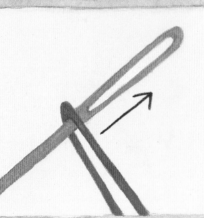

A trick for threading a yarn needle

A trick for getting the soft yarn through the yarn needle's eye is: Wrap the yarn around the eye. Pull it snugly against the edge of the eye until you've created a crease in the yarn. You should be able to slip the flattened, creased yarn into the eye and through.

You've done it! You're now a knitter!

How to fix mistakes

In knitting, it's easy to fix mistakes!

When you find that you've made a mistake, don't panic. There's usually a way to fix it. If there is a hole in your knitting, when the project is finished you can just sew up the hole with yarn. A dropped stitch is a tricky mistake to fix. A dropped stitch is one that has come off your needles and is either just sitting there or is already starting to unravel.

Here's how to fix a dropped stitch:

1. If a stitch has fallen off the needle, sometimes you can just slip it back on.

2. Other times, the stitch might slip off and start unraveling. If this happens, put a safety pin or a short piece of yarn through the dropped stitch to keep it from unraveling more while you're deciding what to do. If a stitch has dropped off the needle and has unraveled several rows, you can simply reweave the stitch, up through your knitting. To reweave the stitch, put a crochet hook through the dropped stitch, hook the stitch directly above it, and pull it through. You now have a new stitch on your crochet hook.

3. Repeat step 2 until you've woven your stitch up through the rows to the top of your knitting, and your dropped stitch is just hanging there. Put the stitch back on your left needle and keep knitting. (Go to my Web site at www.gigiknits.com to watch a video on how to fix an unraveled stitch.)

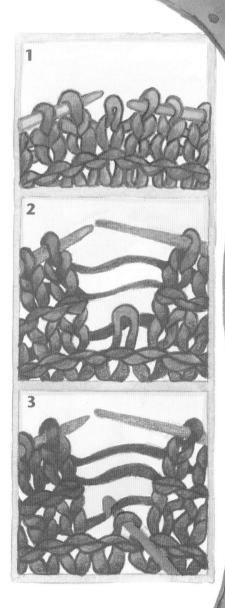

The more you knit, the easier it will be to fix your mistakes!

patterns

Gigi McGreedy has projects galore
Get ready for fun—it's time to explore!

Which one will you do? What will you make first?
A scarf, a belt, or a fabulous purse?

Hats for your friends, for babies or dolls?
You've learned every skill, so just try them all.

First read the pattern and don't skip a bit.
It gives you directions on how you should knit.

Follow it just like a recipe for baking.
But now it's not cookies but clothing you're making.

Next pick out yarn—red, yellow, or blue.
Choose what you like, it's all up to you.

It's finally time for your needles to clack.
So go forth and knit and never look back.

Just use this guide and you'll get a lot done.
Knitting with Gigi is always great fun!

Pot holder

Pot holders make such useful gifts. They're easy, quick, and fun to make. You could make yours with rows of different colors. You can even make them out of leftover yarn.

You will need 1 skein of yarn. I used 100% cotton because it can be machine washed and dried. Be sure to look for worsted weight. Each potholder is about 6 by 6 inches.

1. Cast on 25 stitches.

2. Knit 50 rows (25 garter-stitch ridges) to make a knitted square.

3. Bind off loosely.

4. Weave in the loose ends.

My grandma says, "You can never have too many pot holders."

Holding your yarn as you knit

There are many different ways to hold your yarn as you knit. I hold the yarn between my thumb and index finger. My grandma puts the yarn over her index finger, under her two middle fingers, and then over her little finger. Experiment to see what works best for you.

SAFETY ALERT!

For knitting pot holders, **always** use yarn that is 100% cotton or wool. Among popular yarns, these fibers are the most heat resistant, and so they are the best to use for knitted objects used near flame. Some synthetic yarns can melt near fire and stick to your skin, causing bad burns.

Belt

I love having a great belt to add to an outfit!

This belt is so versatile that last week I wore it as a scarf! I made mine with long fringe.

You will need 1 skein of worsted-weight yarn. I used one that is 55% cotton and 45% acrylic. Machine wash and dry flat.

If you want fringe, cut it before you start your project to make sure you have enough matching yarn. I put the pieces in a plastic bag and kept them in my knitting bag until I was done with the belt, and then attached them to the belt.

1. Cast on 7 stitches. This makes a belt about $1^1/2$ inches wide.

2. Knit about 36 inches or until the belt wraps around your waist, and you can tie it and have some hanging beyond the knot. The belt will stretch a little.

3. Bind off loosely.

4. Weave in loose ends.

5. Attach fringe.

How to make fringe

Fringe is a great way to decorate a purse, scarf, and other things. Here's how you make fringe for the belt:

1. Cut 18 pieces of yarn 20 inches long for each end of the belt.
2. Fold 3 pieces of the fringe in half.
3. On one side of the end of the belt, using a crochet hook, pull the fold of the 3 fringe pieces through the first stitch to form a loop.
4. With the crochet hook, pull all the fringe pieces back through the eye of the loop and tighten.
5. Repeat steps 2 through 4 across the end of the belt 5 more times to the other side.
6. Trim the fringe when you're finished to make it even.

Baby blanket

It's such a great feeling to know that a baby is toasty warm because of something you made for him or her.

To make a baby blanket with 9 squares (each square is about 8 inches on each side), you will need 4 skeins of chunky-weight yarn in the colors of your choice. If you want to make a blanket with 2 colors, you will need 2 skeins of each color. If you want a bigger blanket, get more yarn and make more squares. To make a blanket that's perfect for babies, use a yarn that's warm and easy to clean. The one I used is 75% acrylic and 25% wool. Machine wash and dry.

1. For 1 square, cast on 30 stitches.

2. Knit 60 rows (30 ridges).

3. Bind off loosely.

4. Weave in the loose ends.

5. Repeat steps 1 through 4, until you have 9 squares.

6. To sew the squares together, lay them out on the table the way you want them in the blanket.

7. First, sew the top row of 3 squares together with your yarn needle and brightly colored yarn.

8. Then sew the middle 3 blocks together for the middle row.

9. Sew the final 3 blocks together for the bottom row.

10. Sew the 3 rows together.

Scarves are fun to make because they knit up so fast!

Scarves can be short or very long. They can be skinny or wide. Would your grandma love a skinny glittery scarf for her birthday? Could your dad use a cozy scarf to keep him warm in the snow? I'll give you some ideas for scarves, and then you can be creative. You can make your scarf wider by adding a few extra stitches when you cast on, or you can make it skinnier by casting on fewer stitches.

Skinny glittery scarf

You will need 1 skein of sport-weight yarn, which is enough to make two skinny scarves. Look for a yarn that's pretty but not too slippery to knit. I used one that's mostly nylon with a bit of lamé mixed in. Hand wash and dry flat.

   If you want fringe, cut it first and save it for later. I cut 48 pieces that were each 20 inches long.

1. Cast on 15 stitches.

2. Knit until the scarf is the length you want.

3. Bind off loosely.

4. Weave in loose ends.

5. Add fringe.

Cozy warm scarf

ou need 1 skein of worsted-weight yarn, but get 2 if you want a longer scarf. I wanted a really soft scarf, so I used a yarn that's a blend of alpaca and merino wool. This yarn needs to be hand washed and dried flat. You can use any yarn, but wool is the warmest.

If you want fringe, cut the pieces off first and keep them for later.

1. Cast on 15 stitches.

2. Knit until the scarf is the length you want or the skein is almost gone. Be sure to leave enough yarn to bind off.

3. Bind off loosely.

4. Weave in the ends.

Pocket scarf

If you want to make a scarf with pockets on the ends, here's how:

1. Knit a scarf 8 inches longer than the pattern calls for.
2. Bind off loosely.
3. On each end of the scarf, turn up the ends on the front of the scarf about 4 inches and pin them in place. Sew the side seams for those 4 inches to create a pocket on each end of the scarf.
4. Weave in loose ends.

Experiment!

You could even knit a scarf for your coach in your team's colors. Look on my Web site for the pattern for a two-color scarf. I made a red and blue scarf for my cousin in the Navy, and I added two white felt stars on the ends. He loves it!

Wrist warmers

When my friend Ella got a new winter coat, I made her a matching scarf, wrist warmers, and hat (see pages 30–31). She liked them so much that she made a set for her brother.

You will need 1 skein of worsted-weight yarn. Use one that's acrylic or a blend of acrylic and wool so the wrist warmers can be machine washed and dried.

1. Cast on 25 stitches.

2. Knit 50 rows (25 ridges).

3. Bind off loosely.

4. Repeat steps 1 through 3, making 2 of these square pieces.

5. To sew up the seams of the wrist warmers, lay one of the pieces on the table and position it so that the garter stitch ridges are horizontal (side to side) and not vertical (up and down). The bound-off edge should be at the top and the cast-on edge should be at the bottom.

6. Fold the piece in half, vertically, so that the fold is on the left-hand side.

7. Sew together the top right-hand corners, and sew down about 1 inch of the seam below the corners.

8. Sew together the bottom right-hand corners.

9. Try on the wrist warmer to see where to put the thumbhole. Put your hand through the cylinder. The top sewn seam should be on the inside, or palm, of your hand, underneath your index finger and just above your thumb. You may want to mark the bottom of the thumbhole with a safety pin. I made my thumbhole about 2 inches long.

10. To finish, take off the wrist warmer and sew up the rest of the bottom seam, leaving a thumbhole.

11. Repeat steps 5 through 10 for sewing the second wrist warmer.

12. Weave in loose ends.

Knitting safety

Believe it or not, knitting needles can be dangerous. My friend's mom left her knitting on the front seat of her car and, wow, did she get a surprise when she sat down! Here are a few ways to avoid hurting yourself or someone else with your knitting needles:

- Don't run with knitting needles. If you fall down, you could really get hurt.
- When you're taking a break from knitting, put your needles and project away in a special bag with the needles poked into your yarn ball and pointing down.
- Knitting needles are not toys. Keep them away from babies and anyone who wants to use them in a sword fight. Also keep your needles away from pets who might use them as chew toys.

Everyone can use a really great bag!

I made a bag for my brother's piano books. It's also a perfect size to use as a knitting bag. I also made a bag for my aunt to use for her book club. The bag is about 14 inches wide and 9¹/₂ inches tall.

Bag

You will need 2 skeins of chunky-weight yarn that is a blend of acrylic and wool. Machine wash and dry. If you want to make a lining, you will need ¹/₂ yard of any washable fabric, matching thread, and a sewing needle.

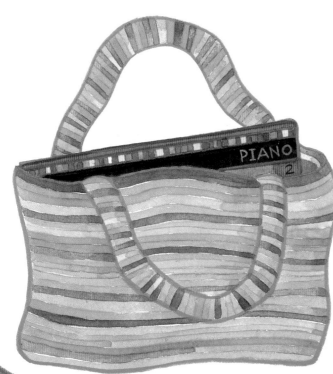

1. Start by making the straps. Cast on 8 stitches.

2. Knit 14 inches.

3. Bind off loosely.

4. Repeat to make 2 straps and set aside.

5. For the bag, cast on 50 stitches.

6. Knit every row for about 20 inches or until the piece is twice as tall as you want the bag to be.

7. Bind off loosely, leaving a long tail to sew up your seam.

8. Lay the knitted piece on the table so that the garter stitch ridges are horizontal (side by side), not vertical.

9. To make a lining for the bag, cut the fabric the same size as the knitted piece. Press a ¹/₂-inch hem under on all sides. Pin the fabric to the knitted piece to make sure it's just where you want it, with the hem folded under. Now sew the long sides of the fabric in place with a needle and thread.

10. To sew the knitted piece into a bag shape, fold the bag in half by taking the bottom corners and bringing them up to the top corners. (If your bag has a lining, it should be on the inside.) Sew together the side seams. Weave in loose ends.

11. To position the straps, use safety pins. On the front of the bag, take the first strap and position each end about 2 inches from the side seams. You can put the strap ends on the outside of the bag or on the inside—your choice. Pin each strap end in place, making sure the strap is not twisted.

12. Using your yarn needle and some extra yarn, sew about 1 inch of each end of the strap securely to the front of the bag.

13. To make the strap stronger, fold the section between the ends in half and stitch the edges together.

14. On the back of the bag, repeat this process with the second strap.

15. If you have made a lining, sew the top of the lining to the inside of the bag with a needle and thread.

Patterns for purse and cell phone case

I made a purse for myself using a smaller version of this pattern. It has a pocket on the outside and braided straps. When my friends tell me how cute my purse is, it's fun to be able to say that I made it myself! I also made a cell phone case, using an even smaller version of this pattern, with an added flap and a cute button. See my Web site for the purse pattern and the cell phone case pattern.

Hat

This hat can go with the wrist warmers, as a set!

You can make this hat plain, or with a rolled-up brim. It is perfect for anyone.

You will need at least 1 skein of worsted-weight yarn that is a blend of acrylic and wool. Machine wash and dry.

1. Cast on 72 stitches.

2. Knit 6 inches if you want a hat without a brim. Knit 8 inches if you want to turn up the bottom and make a brim.

3. To make the top of the hat smaller, start with a row when the tail is at the lower left of your knitted piece, like in the picture below. Decrease 6 stitches as follows: Knit 10 stitches, knit 2 together, knit 10 stitches, knit 2 together, knit 10 stitches, knit 2 together, knit 10 stitches, knit 2 together, knit 10 stitches, knit 2 together, knit 10 stitches, knit 2 together. You should now have 66 stitches.

4. Knit 3 rows.

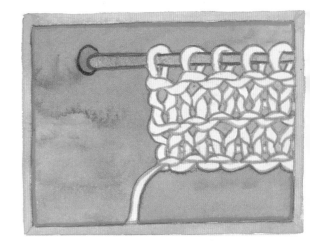

5. The tail should be at the lower left corner of your knitting. Repeat the following for the entire row: Knit 4 stitches, knit 2 together. You should now have 55 stitches.

6. Knit 1 row.

7. The tail should be at the lower left corner of your knitting. Repeat the following for the entire row: Knit 3 stitches, knit 2 together. You should now have 44 stitches.

8. Knit 1 row.

9. The tail should be at the lower left. Repeat the following for the entire row: Knit 2 stitches, knit 2 together. You should now have 33 stitches.

10. Knit 1 row.

11. The tail should be at the lower left. Repeat the following for the entire row: Knit 1 stitch, knit 2 together. You should now have 22 stitches.

12. Knit 1 row.

13. The tail should be at the lower left. Repeat the following for the entire row: Knit 2 together. You should now have 11 stitches.

14. Cut your yarn, leaving an 18-inch tail.

15. Thread the tail through the eye of a yarn needle. Run the needle through the remaining stitches as you take the stitches off the needle. Pull tight.

16. To sew the back seam, line up the edges together and pin them so they are even. Starting at the top of the hat, use the long tail to sew the seam with your yarn needle. After you're done sewing the seam, turn it inside out and check it for holes. Use extra yarn to sew holes closed and firm up the seam from the inside.

17. For a rolled-brim hat, you may not want the seam to show at the bottom. When sewing the seam shut, when you are about 1 inch from the bottom of the hat, sew your seam on the inside instead of on the outside, so the seam won't show when it is rolled up.

18. Weave in any remaining loose ends.

See my Web site, for other hat patterns for babies and adults.

knitting to help others

Knitting is a great way to show people you care.

Gigi McGreedy requests your assistance
To change the whole world with cheerful
persistence.

She hopes caring people will simply not say,
"I am simply too busy to help others today."

So let's all pitch in and develop a plan
To help someone else and do all that we can.

It won't take too long and we will discover
How nice it feels when we do things for others.

We won't need prizes or treasure to store.
Kindness to others is its own great reward.

There are many organizations in your
community that might love to receive
knitted items. Check with your local
hospital, homeless shelter, domestic
violence shelter, senior center, or even the
animal shelter. Some organizations are
Binky Patrol, Care Wear, Warm Up
America!, Helping Hands Foundation,
Hugs for Homeless Animals, Magic
Mittens and Mufflers for Mongolian
Children, and Project Linus. See my Web
site, www.gigiknits.com, for contact
information on organizations that accept
knitting donations.

You can make a difference!

Visit www.gigiknits.com for more patterns and instructions!